MAKE YOUR OWN
BILTONG AND DROËWORS

MAKE YOUR OWN

BILTONG AND DROËWORS

Compiled by Hannelie van Tonder
Photography by Willie van Heerden

STRUIK

Acknowledgements

The Publisher wishes to thank Kurt Rietmann of
Kurt Rietmann (Pty) Ltd, Maitland,
for supplying the photographs on pages 38, 39, and 48.

Struik Publishers (Pty) Ltd
(a member of Struik New Holland Publishing (Pty) Ltd)
Cornelis Struik House
80 McKenzie Street
Cape Town 8001

Reg. No.: 54/00965/07

First published by Struik Timmins in February 1991
3 5 7 9 10 8 6 4 2
This edition published by Struik Publishers in 1992
9 10 8

Copyright © Meat Board 1991, 1992

Compiled by Hannelie van Tonder of the Meat Board in
collaboration with the red meat industry of South Africa.

Editor: Linda de Villiers
Designer: Janice Evans
Design assistant: Lellyn Creamer
Illustrator: Marianne Saddington
Photographer: Willie van Heerden
Stylist: Gay Mitchell and Nelda Andringa, and assisted by
Ria Esterhuizen
Props: Myrna Klerck

Typesetting by Diatype Setting cc, Cape Town
Reproduction by Unifoto (Pty) Ltd, Cape Town
Printed and bound by Kyodo Printing Co (Singapore) Pte Ltd

ISBN 1 86825 289 2

Contents

Introduction

Meat Board senior home economist, Hannelie van Tonder, believes that there is renewed interest in the traditional processes of making biltong, sausages and cured and smoked meats. With the aid of full colour photographs and step-by-step instructions, Hannelie has made it possible for everyone to master these methods at home.

Biltong is delicious eaten as a snack but try it in quiches, muffins, bread, sandwiches and salads as an appetizing alternative. Learn to make South Africa's spicy sausage, boerewors, as well as droëwors, salami, liver, pork and Russian sausages. Teamed with other ingredients, these sausages make tasty dishes for breakfasts, lunches and suppers.

Although usually carried out by large commercial enterprises, the processes of curing and smoking meat can easily be undertaken at home. Simply follow the concise instructions and produce your own mouth-watering hams, bacon, 'soutribbetjies' and corned beef.

As busy as our lives are today, some things cannot be rushed – biltong, sausages and cured and smoked meats are best made the old traditional way.

Biltong

For most South Africans, these strips of salted, dried beef still remain the tastiest snack. This popular delicacy is synonymous with tradition and, although various forms of 'biltong' are found in other countries, nowhere is it found in exactly the same form as we know it here. In the past farmers used a whole beef carcase for biltong and sausages but today the beef buttock, consisting of the silverside (from which 'ronde-' or 'predikantsbiltong' and 'regte biltong' are made), topside and thick flank, is normally used. The finest biltong is the 'garingbiltong' made from the eye muscles running down both sides of the backbone and which are cut whole from a side of beef. The most tender is the 'binnebiltong' or 'ouma se biltong' which is made from the fillet. Less tender cuts such as chuck can also be used, but the pieces of biltong will be small and much time will have to be spent on removing the connective tissue.

Whichever cuts you decide to use, ensure that the meat is of good quality: lean cuts from a young carcase containing little fat, are best (excess fat on the biltong will cause rancidity). Fatty meat takes a long time to absorb the salt while biltong made from an old carcase is tough and sinewy.

BEEF

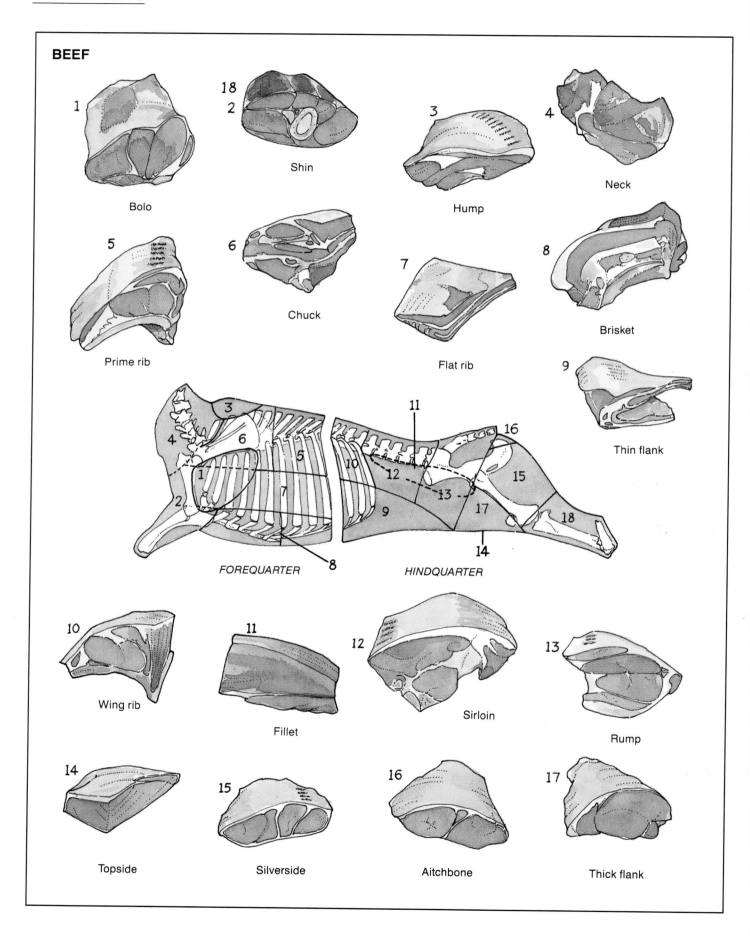

1 Bolo

18
2 Shin

3 Hump

4 Neck

5 Prime rib

6 Chuck

7 Flat rib

8 Brisket

9 Thin flank

FOREQUARTER   HINDQUARTER

10 Wing rib

11 Fillet

12 Sirloin

13 Rump

14 Topside

15 Silverside

16 Aitchbone

17 Thick flank

When making biltong use good quality meat and remove as much connective tissue as possible.

CUTTING THE MEAT

Remove as much connective tissue as possible and cut the meat into long strips ranging in width from 25-50 mm. The thickness of the strips is a matter of personal preference but in more humid areas it would be necessary to cut thinner strips. Use a large, sharp knife to make neat, clean incisions into the meat – loose pieces of meat can cause mould to set in.

SALTING

The basic recipe for biltong is 200-400 g dairy salt to every 10 kg meat. Bear in mind that the longer the meat remains in the salt, the more salt is absorbed and that the longer the biltong is left to dry, the more salty it will become.

Although it is common practice to use only salt or salt and pepper, many biltong makers have their own special blends. Other ingredients such as brown sugar can be added as this counteracts the toughening effect of salt, resulting in more tender biltong. It is used in small quantities and does not sweeten the biltong. Bicarbonate of soda is sometimes added to prevent mould forming on biltong made in more humid areas. Pepper and freshly scorched and ground coriander add flavour while saltpetre gives beef biltong its characteristic red colour. Other spices such as aniseed, garlic salt and allspice can also be added but should never overpower the flavour of the meat.

TO SCORCH CORIANDER
Place the seeds in a dry frying pan and heat, stirring constantly, until they become light brown. Grind them in a blender or with a pestle and mortar, or crush them between two pieces of cloth using a rolling pin. Pass the crushed seeds through a sieve to remove the husks. Crush 15 mℓ whole coriander to obtain 5 mℓ ground coriander.

After cutting the meat, weigh it and, referring to the table given below, calculate the quantity of salt and other ingredients needed. Rub the salt or salt mixture into the meat and place it in a suitable container, putting the thicker pieces at the bottom and the thinner strips on top. Sprinkle a little vinegar over and leave overnight.

BASIC RECIPE			OPTIONAL ADDITIONS		
MEAT	SALT	SUGAR	SALTPETRE	BICARBONATE OF SODA	PEPPER
25 kg	500 g-1 kg (500 mℓ-1ℓ)	180 g (225 mℓ)	20 g (15 mℓ)	20 g (25 mℓ)	15 mℓ
50 kg	1-2 kg (1-2 ℓ)	350 g (450 mℓ)	40 g (25 mℓ)	40 g (50 mℓ)	12 g (25 mℓ)

SPICES (USE ONLY ONE IN COMBINATION WITH THE PEPPER)					
MEAT	ANISEED	CORIANDER	ALLSPICE	GARLIC SALT	
25 kg	100 g (350 mℓ)	80-160 g (200-400 mℓ)	5 mℓ	15 mℓ	
50 kg	180 g (625 mℓ)	160-320 g (400-800 mℓ)	7 mℓ	20 mℓ	

When drying biltong indoors, make sure there is a draught by using an electric fan to create a good air-flow.

CONTAINERS

Use plastic, stainless steel, enamel or earthenware containers for the salting of the meat. Metal containers or even chipped enamel ones are unsuitable as the salt mixture reacts to the metal, discolouring the meat and giving it a bad taste.

DRYING

Dip the strips of meat into hot vinegar water (350 mℓ to 5 ℓ boiling water) to remove the surface salt and, using thin hooks or string loops, hang up the strips of meat. Hang them well apart so that they do not touch one another, otherwise mould will set in. Allow the strips to sun-dry for the first day, then move them to the shade for the rest of the drying period, two to three weeks. Biltong can be hung indoors, but make sure there is a draught – an electric fan can be used to create a good air-flow.

YIELD

During the drying process, about 50-60% of the meat mass is lost, which means that only about 40% of the original weight will be left over as biltong. For example, a 25 kg buttock will yield only about 10 kg of biltong.

STORING BILTONG

Beef biltong is at its best when the inside is soft, moist and red in colour, with a hard brown outer layer. To keep it from drying out further, wrap the biltong in cling wrap, squeeze out all the air, and deep-freeze it indefinitely. Thaw biltong overnight in the refrigerator, and then at room temperature for 1 hour.

If you prefer dry biltong, store it in a cool, dry place where it can be kept for many years (the fat may go rancid with time but the meat will keep). Dry biltong can also be stored in a muslin bag, which allows free air circulation. Never store dry biltong in plastic. Freeze grated biltong in plastic bags or airtight plastic containers but remember to bring it to room temperature before serving – biltong has very little taste if it is too cold.

BILTONG-MAKERS

Most household biltong-makers work on the principle of convection with an electric globe creating the perfect conditions for drying the meat within three to five days. These appliances usually consist of a cardboard box with a loose-bottomed end into which a 40-watt bulb is fitted. Up to 5 kg of meat can be hung from the galvanized rods which fit into special notches in the top of the unit. These biltong-makers come complete with the manufacturer's instructions and are easy to assemble.

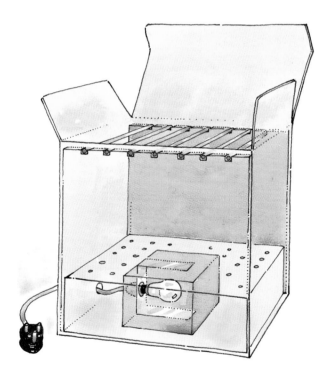

An example of a typical household biltong-maker which works on the principle of convection. A 40 watt electric bulb creates the perfect conditions for drying the meat within three to five days.

HINTS
- Cut the meat into slightly smaller strips if it is to be dried in a biltong-maker
- Do not hang up more than 5 kg of meat at one time
- Use the standard biltong recipe given on page 11

STEP BY STEP

1. Choose lean cuts of meat for biltong-making, for example, silverside, thick flank and topside.

2. Cut the meat with the grain into long strips, as thick as you wish (usually 25-50 mm).

3. Place the meat to a suitable container and sprinkle each layer with the salt mixture.

4. Sprinkle with a little brown vinegar and leave overnight in a cool place.

5. The next day, dip the strips of meat into hot vinegar water to remove surface salt.

6. Hang the meat from wire hooks or string loops in a cool, draughty place to dry.

BILTONG POTBREAD

DOUGH
240 g cake flour (500 mℓ)
20 mℓ baking powder
2 mℓ salt
5 mℓ mustard powder
100 g butter
approximately 100 mℓ milk
1 egg, beaten

FILLING
120 g grated biltong (250 mℓ)
200 g smooth cottage cheese
15 mℓ lemon juice
30 mℓ chopped parsley
freshly ground black pepper to taste
mayonnaise to moisten

To make the dough: Sift together the dry ingredients. Cut the butter into the flour with a knife and then rub it in with your fingertips until the mixture resembles dried breadcrumbs.

Beat the milk and egg together. Make a well in the flour mixture and add the liquid gradually. Mix quickly to a soft dough. Turn out onto a floured board and knead lightly until smooth. Roll out into a square approximately 10 mm thick.

To make the filling: Mix all ingredients together and spread over the dough, keeping 25 mm clear along the edges. Roll up the dough like a Swiss roll, and seal the edges with beaten egg and water. Wrap lightly in greaseproof paper and refrigerate for about 30 minutes. Carefully cut the dough into 25-mm slices and arrange them, cut side down, on the bottom of a greased No. 3 flat-bottomed cast-iron pot. Begin in the centre and arrange the remaining slices in a circle. Leave the sides of the pot clear to allow the dough to rise. Grease the inside of the lid with cooking oil or butter and cover the pot. Put the pot over a small fire, place a few small, hot coals on the lid and bake for 20-30 minutes or until the bread is golden brown and cooked. Turn out, cool slightly, then serve with crisp vegetable sticks and lettuce leaves.
SERVES 6

BILTONG SPREAD

125 g smooth cream cheese with chives
30 mℓ mayonnaise
30 mℓ lemon juice
30 mℓ chopped parsley
60 g grated biltong (125 mℓ)
salt and freshly ground black pepper to taste

Combine all the ingredients and serve sandwiched between slices of bread and toasted in an electric sandwich-maker * spread on slices of wholewheat bread and garnished with thin slices of lemon or cucumber * spread on bread canapés: cut slices of bread into rounds or fingers, fry in heated cooking oil until golden brown. Cool on a wire rack, then spread with biltong mixture and garnish with sliced olives or gherkins.
MAKES ABOUT 300 Mℓ

BILTONG MUFFINS

120 g wholewheat flour (250 mℓ)
120 g cake flour (250 mℓ)
200 g biltong, finely chopped (500 mℓ)
50 g Cheddar cheese (125 mℓ)
30 mℓ baking powder
3 eggs
200 mℓ milk
100 mℓ cooking oil
5 mℓ salt
15 mℓ lemon juice

Combine all ingredients and mix lightly. Spoon into greased muffin pans and bake at 220 °C for 11 minutes. Leave to cool slightly before removing and serving with butter.
MAKES 12

From left to right: Biltong potbread, Biltong spread and Biltong muffins

BILTONG AND CHEESE QUICHE

PASTRY
150 g cake flour (300 mℓ)
2 mℓ salt
5 mℓ mustard powder
120 g butter
50 mℓ ice water

FILLING
2 leeks, sliced
15 mℓ butter
15 mℓ cooking oil
30 mℓ chopped fennel leaves or parsley
120 g grated biltong or strips of moist beef biltong (250 mℓ)
4 eggs, beaten
250 mℓ cream
125 mℓ sour cream
100 g grated Cheddar cheese (250 mℓ)
5 mℓ mustard powder
15 mℓ lemon juice
5 mℓ grated lemon rind
freshly ground black pepper to taste

To make the pastry: Sift together the flour, salt and mustard. Cut butter into small cubes, add to flour and rub in lightly with fingertips. Gradually add water, mixing to a soft dough. Turn out onto a pastry board and shape into a smooth ball. Place the dough in a plastic bag or cling wrap and refrigerate for at least 30 minutes. Roll out on a floured pastry board and line a 230-mm diameter quiche dish. Refrigerate for a further 30 minutes, then bake blind (see Box below).

To make the filling: Sauté the leeks in heated butter and cooking oil until transparent. Scatter leeks on the base of the pastry case. Mix remaining ingredients and pour into pastry case. Bake at 160 °C for 35-45 minutes until set.
SERVES 8

TO BAKE PASTRY SHELLS BLIND
Line the dough with greaseproof paper and fill with dried beans or rice. Bake in a pre-heated 200 °C oven for 8-9 minutes. Lift out paper with beans or rice, return shell to oven and bake for a further 5 minutes.

BILTONG STARTER WITH LEMON FENNEL SAUCE

250 g biltong, thinly sliced (500 mℓ)

FRENCH SALAD DRESSING
30 mℓ wine vinegar or lemon juice
60 mℓ olive or salad oil
5 mℓ salt
freshly ground black pepper to taste
30 mℓ chopped parsley
30 mℓ chopped spring onion

LEMON FENNEL SAUCE
150 mℓ mayonnaise
150 mℓ sour cream
5 mℓ chopped fennel leaves
1 small onion, grated
15 mℓ chopped parsley
15 mℓ lemon juice
1 mℓ mustard powder
salt and pepper to taste

GARNISH
small butter lettuce leaves
red pepper, cut into strips

Mix ingredients for French salad dressing and pour over biltong slices. Marinate for 4-6 hours. Combine all ingredients for lemon fennel sauce. Arrange 4-6 slices of biltong in a fan on each plate and garnish with lettuce leaves and red pepper. Spoon a little sauce onto each plate and serve.
SERVES 10-12

BILTONG SALAD

a few young spinach leaves
a few cos lettuce leaves
a few red butter lettuce leaves
250 g thin slices moist beef biltong
2 hard-boiled eggs, quartered
30 mℓ chopped parsley
approximately 125 mℓ bean sprouts or small bunch watercress
250 mℓ croûtons

FRENCH DRESSING
30 mℓ wine vinegar or lemon juice
60 mℓ olive or salad oil or a mixture of both
5 mℓ salt
freshly ground white pepper to taste
5 mℓ mustard powder
pinch sugar (optional)
2 cloves garlic, chopped
15 mℓ chopped parsley or fresh herbs

Toss all the leaves together lightly. Add remaining ingredients, except croûtons and dressing, and toss lightly.
   Make the dressing by combining all the ingredients in a screw-top jar. Just before serving, shake the dressing well and drizzle over salad ingredients. Toss lightly, then scatter croûtons over. Serve with hot, buttered scones.
SERVES 4

Biltong salad (left), Biltong and cheese quiche (foreground) and Biltong starter with lemon fennel sauce (right)

Sausages

Sausage-making is a very old form of food preservation — it is believed that sausages have been made for as long as animals have been slaughtered for food. Although some sausages were eaten fresh, some types were spiced to help prolong their life for a few days, or dried and preserved for later use. Today, the making of sausages differs from country to country and from region to region. This difference may be due to the type and coarseness of the meat, the proportion of fat to lean meat and the addition of spices and seasonings. Even the casings used tend to differ and may be pork, beef, mutton or cellulose.

The making of boerewors and droëwors, sausages peculiar to South Africa, has become an art-form. This coarse, loose-textured sausage is flavoured with spices such as coriander, cloves, nutmeg and allspice, but the kind of seasoning used is often influenced by the area in which the boerewors is made. We have provided no less than four variations which can serve as the starting point for the development of your own personal boerewors recipe.

The softly-lit interior of a German delicatessen where an array of sausages, hams and other cured and smoked meats are displayed.

THE MEAT

Use fresh, not frozen, beef, pork, mutton or combinations of these meats, together with speck or sheep's tail fat. Although top grade meat is not essential, the tough connective tissue must be removed before mincing. Use meat from young animals as the meat from older animals tends to affect the colour and binding quality of the sausage. Never wash the meat with water as this causes spoilage and a tough texture.

Boerewors

When making boerewors, use 6 parts meat to 1 part speck. The beef/pork ratio is a matter of taste, but two parts beef to one part pork will give an appetizing end result. Cut the meat into 50-mm cubes, spread them on a clean surface, sprinkle the spices over and mix *very lightly*. Dice the speck into 3-mm cubes or if you have a special coarse mincer plate it can be minced separately. Mince the meat, adding a sprinkling of speck to each layer of mince. The object here is to get a mixture of mince and speck without too much handling as overhandling results in a polony-like texture. Boerewors should have a loose, fairly coarse texture and it is important, therefore, to make sure that the mincer blade and plate are sharp and to use a mincer plate with large (9 mm) holes. Finer holes will result in a texture that is too firm.

SPECK

This is pork fat usually cut in slabs from the belly of a baconer. It is easier to cut it into slices, squares or dice if it is placed in the freezer for about 30 minutes before use.

Droëwors

This is made in much the same way as boerewors *(see page 21)* except that pork and speck are not used (pork fat tends to go rancid). Saltpetre may be added as a preservative but will give the meat a reddish colour.

Dip the filled sausage casings in boiling water to which a good measure of vinegar has been added (350 mℓ to 4,5 ℓ of water). Hang the lengths of sausage over wooden poles thick enough to keep the inner surfaces from touching – don't use wire hooks as these could pierce the casings.

After a day, flatten the partially dried wors to get rid of any air bubbles where mould may set in. (If the casings are filled loosely, they will flatten more easily.)

To improve the flavour, droëwors may be smoked *(see page 37)* after a day of hanging. Droëwors and smoked droëwors can be frozen for up to two months in an airtight container or wrapped in cling wrap.

THE SPICES

These should be used with discretion so as not to overpower the flavour of the meat. Salt and pepper are the main seasonings for almost all sausages although coriander is the most common spice used for traditional boerewors. To bring out the flavour, coriander should be scorched, ground and sieved *(see page 11)*. If whole coriander is not available, use ground coriander (5 mℓ ground coriander for every 15 mℓ whole coriander required in the recipe).

Other popular additions include ground cloves, nutmeg and crushed garlic. Herbs such as thyme and marjoram give an interesting flavour but, like spices, should be used sparingly.

SAUSAGE CASINGS

These are obtainable from spice dealers and butchers and can be pork (available fresh or preserved in salt), beef, mutton or cellulose. If preserved in salt, casings must be soaked in lukewarm water for about 30 minutes, then rinsed in cold running water before use. Unused casings can again be preserved in salt and stored in the refrigerator or freezer.

Pork casings are the best for boerewors while mutton rather than pork casings should be used for mutton sausages and if you prefer thinner sausages.

When filling the casings, especially at the start of each new casing, press out all the accumulating air to prevent air bubbles forming but never fill the casing too tightly as this will cause it to burst during cooking.

STORING SAUSAGES

Before using or freezing, keep fresh sausages in the refrigerator for at least a day to dry out the casing and to allow the flavours to permeate the meat thoroughly.

Uncooked boerewors can be stored in the refrigerator for a day or two while cooked wors can be placed in well-sealed, sterilized bottles and covered with clean fat. This method of preserving is particularly popular with campers.

Fresh sausages can be frozen for up to two months after which time the flavour may change.

COOKING SAUSAGES

It is important to cook your homemade sausages correctly. Place them in an unheated, riffle pan without the addition of cooking oil or any liquid. Heat slowly and, without pricking the skin, turn the sausages to brown on all sides until pan-grilled to taste.

STEP-BY-STEP

1. Cut the meat into 50-mm cubes, sprinkle with combined seasonings and mix to coat.

2. Remove the rind and cut the speck into long thin strips; then cube or dice.

3. Mince the meat, using a 9 mm plate, and add a little of the speck to each layer of mince.

4. Soak the casings in lukewarm water for about 30 minutes, rinse with cold running water, and pull over sausage filler.

5. Stuff casing with minced meat – don't overfill and avoid getting air in.

6. Refrigerate for at least 24 hours before cooking in a riffle pan, or freezing.

TRADITIONAL BOEREWORS

This recipe took the first prize in a country-wide boerewors competition. Try it – it's delicious!

2 kg beef
1 kg pork
20 g whole coriander (50 mℓ)
2 mℓ ground cloves
2 mℓ grated nutmeg
30 g fine salt (25 mℓ)
5 mℓ freshly ground black pepper
500 g speck
100 mℓ vinegar
approximately 90 g casings

First prepare the coriander by scorching, grinding and sifting it *(see page 11)*. Cut the meat into 50-mm cubes and combine with the spices and seasoning. Mince the meat and dice the speck. Add speck and vinegar to the minced meat and mix lightly but thoroughly. Loosely stuff mixture into the casings.
MAKES ABOUT 3,5 KG

BOEREWORS
(bulk quantity)

40 kg beef
20 kg pork (not too lean)
1 kg speck
1 kg fine salt
500 g whole coriander
25 mℓ freshly ground black pepper
25 mℓ ground cloves
25 mℓ grated nutmeg
1,1 ℓ vinegar
1 kg casings

First prepare the coriander by scorching, grinding and sifting it *(see page 11)*. Cut the meat and speck into 50-mm cubes, spread on a clean working surface and sprinkle with remaining ingredients, except vinegar and casings. Mix together lightly, and then mince. Add vinegar, mix lightly, then loosely fill the casings with the mixture.
MAKES ABOUT 64 KG

KAROO BOEREWORS

500 g beef
500 g pork
1 kg mutton
1 mℓ ground coriander
1 mℓ ground cloves
14 g fine salt (15 mℓ)
2 mℓ freshly ground black pepper
250 g speck
15 mℓ sweet red wine
25 mℓ wine vinegar
15 mℓ brandy
60 g casings

Cut the meat into 50-mm cubes, sprinkle with the spices and seasonings and mince. Dice the speck into 3-mm cubes and sprinkle over meat. Combine red wine, vinegar and brandy and sprinkle over meat mixture. Mix lightly, then stuff loosely into casings.
MAKES ABOUT 2,5 KG

MUTTON SAUSAGE

5 kg mutton
500 g sheep's tail fat (if mutton is lean)
30-55 g fine salt (25-50 mℓ)
10 mℓ freshly ground white pepper
10 g ground coriander (25 mℓ)
10 g allspice (20-25 mℓ)
150 mℓ white vinegar
400 mℓ Worcestershire sauce
90 g casings

Cut the meat and sheep's tail fat into 50-mm cubes. Mix all seasoning and spices together and add to meat. Mince the meat mixture, sprinkle with vinegar and Worcestershire sauce and mix lightly but thoroughly. Loosely stuff mixture into the casings. Mutton sausages can also be dried *(see Droëwors on page 20)*.
MAKES ABOUT 6 KG

NOTE
☐ Traditionally mutton sausages are thin and, therefore, mutton casings should be used.

PORK SAUSAGE

3 kg pork
30 g fine salt (25 mℓ)
5 mℓ freshly ground white pepper
2 mℓ ground cloves
15 mℓ whole coriander
2 mℓ grated nutmeg
150 mℓ vinegar
90 g casings

First prepare the coriander by scorching, grinding and sifting it *(see page 11)*. Cut the meat into 50-mm cubes and combine with remaining ingredients, except vinegar and casings. Mince the meat, add vinegar and mix lightly but thoroughly. Loosely stuff the mixture into the casings, then twist the casing to form sausages 10 cm in length.
MAKES 3 KG

NOTE
☐ For a finer texture, mince the meat mixture twice.

LIVER SAUSAGE

2,5 kg pork, beef or mutton liver
2,5 kg pork
1,5 kg speck
30 g fine salt (25 mℓ)
7 mℓ ground cloves
7 mℓ grated nutmeg
10 mℓ freshly ground black pepper
180 g casings

Pull the thin veil of membrane away from the liver. Using a small, sharp knife, cut out the veins, then cube the liver. Half cover with water and simmer until tender, then drain. Cube the pork and speck, half cover with water and simmer until tender. Combine the drained pork and speck with the liver and spices and mince twice. Stuff into casings, then twist the casing to form sausages 15-20 cm in length. Place sausages in boiling water and simmer for 5 minutes.
MAKES ABOUT 7 KG

VARIATION
Instead of filling the casings, the mixture can be spooned into sterilized bottles and refrigerated for use as a spread or as a vol-au-vent filling.

RUSSIAN SAUSAGES

2,5 kg lean beef
4,8 kg fatty pork
1 kg Russian spice and curing salt *(see Note below)*
1 kg iced water
pork casings

Mince the beef, using a 3 mm mincing plate. Cube the pork and set aside. Mix the curing salt with the beef and leave overnight. Add the spice, iced water and pork and mix well. Mince all the ingredients together using a 4,5 mm plate and stuff into 28-32 mm pork casings. Twist the casings to form sausages 10 cm in length.

To smoke the sausages: Hang them in the smoker and smoke at a medium temperature for 20-30 minutes. Lower the sausages so that they are closer to the heat, add more sawdust and smoke with increased heat for a further 30-40 minutes until brick colour. Cook in water at 72 °C (use a temperature probe) for 20 minutes, then cool down with iced water. Hang up to dry, then refrigerate.
MAKES ABOUT 10 KG

NOTE
☐ Russian spice and curing salt is available from spice dealers.

GERMAN SALAMI

Salami should not be made during the hot summer months since mould and decay may set in.

5 kg pork
5 kg boned chuck
160 g fine salt (140 mℓ)
10 mℓ saltpetre
60 g sugar (75 mℓ)
10 mℓ freshly ground white pepper
1 clove garlic, crushed
casings *(see Note)*

Cut meat into 50-mm cubes and sprinkle with salt, saltpetre and sugar. Leave for a while to draw water. Mince the meat, add pepper and garlic and mix lightly but thoroughly. Dip the casings into water, then stuff with the meat mixture. Tie off at 50-cm intervals with thin string, drawing it tightly to give a scalloped effect. Hang the salami for 24 hours at room temperature to dry, then smoke the sausage *(see page 37)* and hang it up for 10-14 days to ripen.
MAKES ABOUT 10 KG

NOTE
☐ Special thick, 50-mm diameter salami casings should be used.
☐ Do not use synthetic casings as air cannot circulate through the casings and mould will set in.
☐ For your convenience, special salami spice mixtures can be obtained from spice dealers.

FARM-STYLE DROËWORS

4,5 kg beef
2,5 kg breast of mutton/fatty mutton
15 mℓ freshly ground black pepper
15 mℓ ground cloves
15 mℓ grated nutmeg
12 g whole coriander (30 mℓ)
90 g fine salt (75 mℓ)
15 mℓ brown sugar
400 mℓ vinegar
90 g mutton or pork casings

First prepare the coriander by scorching, grinding and sifting it *(see page 11)*. Cut the beef and breast of mutton/fatty mutton into 50-mm cubes, mix with the remaining ingredients, except the vinegar and casings, and mince. Sprinkle vinegar over the minced meat mixture and mix lightly. Stuff the mixture loosely into the casings. Dip the sausages in a mixture of 4,5 ℓ boiling water and 350 mℓ vinegar, then hang over wooden rods thick enough to prevent the inner surfaces from touching. Dry in a cool, draughty place for 24 hours, then flatten to expel the air. Leave hanging until sausages are completely dried.

MAKES ABOUT 4 KG

From left to right: Liver sausage, Russian sausages and German salami

TRADITIONAL DROËWORS

4,5 kg beef or mutton
1 kg sheep's tail fat
34 g fine salt (30 mℓ)
20 g whole coriander (50 mℓ)
5 mℓ ground cloves
10 mℓ freshly ground black pepper
90 g casings *(see Note)*

First prepare the coriander by scorching, grinding and sifting it *(see page 11)*. Cut the beef or mutton and sheep's tail fat into 50-mm cubes and combine with the remaining ingredients. Mince together, then loosely stuff into casings. Dip the sausages into a mixture of 4,5 ℓ boiling water and 350 mℓ vinegar, then hang over wooden rods thick enough to prevent the inner surfaces from touching. Dry in a cool, draughty place for 24 hours, then flatten to expel the air. Leave hanging until sausages are completely dried.

MAKES ABOUT 3 KG

NOTE
☐ Use mutton casings when making mutton sausages.

HINT
● Droëwors can also be smoked *(see page 37)* after hanging for a day. Not only does smoking give droëwors a delicious flavour, but it also draws more moisture out of the meat and destroys mould and micro-organisms.

WORS WITH RATATOUILLE

300 g boerewors

RATATOUILLE
1 onion, finely chopped
15 mℓ cooking oil
2 tomatoes, skinned and cubed
1 brinjal, sliced
125 g baby marrows, sliced
5 mℓ salt
1 mℓ freshly ground black pepper
2 mℓ dried oregano

Place the boerewors in a cold riffle pan. Heat gradually and grill until almost done. Put aside and keep warm. Sauté the onion in heated cooking oil. Add tomatoes, brinjal, baby marrows and seasonings and simmer slowly until tender. Add boerewors and simmer together for approximately 5 minutes.
SERVES 4

VARIATION
Add sliced mushrooms, green pepper and crushed garlic for a delicious variation.

TOAD-IN-THE-HOLE

250 g rindless bacon
250 g boerewors, cut into small portions

BATTER
120 g cake flour (250 mℓ)
2 mℓ salt
2 eggs, beaten
200 mℓ milk
50 mℓ water

Roll bacon into small tight rolls and pin with cocktail sticks. Place the boerewors and bacon in an ovenproof dish and bake in a preheated 200 °C oven for 10 minutes. Remove and discard cocktail sticks from bacon.
  Make the batter by sifting together the cake flour and salt. Beat eggs, milk and water, pour into well in flour and mix to a smooth batter. Refrigerate for approximately 30 minutes, beat well, and then pour over boerewors and bacon. Return dish to oven and bake at 200 °C for 30 minutes until golden brown.
SERVES 4

BOEREWORS WITH MUSTARD POTATOES

500 g boerewors
4 large potatoes
4 rashers rindless bacon
1 onion, chopped
1 clove garlic, crushed
2 gherkins, chopped

MUSTARD SAUCE
1 egg yolk
125 mℓ mayonnaise
15 mℓ prepared mustard
30 mℓ chopped parsley or fresh herbs

First prepare the mustard sauce: Beat egg yolk until foamy. Add mayonnaise spoon by spoon, beating until ingredients are well blended. Lastly add mustard and parsley or herbs. Refrigerate in an air-tight container until required.

Pan-grill the boerewors until done, set aside and keep warm. Boil potatoes in their jackets until tender, then peel and cube while still hot. Fry bacon in frying pan until crisp, add onion and garlic and sauté. Add warm bacon mixture, gherkins and mustard sauce to potatoes and mix lightly. Serve the boerewors with the mustard potatoes.
SERVES 6

Wors with ratatouille (left), Russian sausage and banana kebabs (right) and Boerewors with mustard potatoes (foreground)

OMELETTE DELIGHT

1 onion, chopped
15 mℓ cooking oil
4 eggs, beaten
15 mℓ chopped parsley
salt and freshly ground black pepper to taste
150 g cooked boerewors, sliced

Sauté the onion in heated cooking oil in a heavy-based frying pan. Beat the eggs, parsley and seasonings together and pour into pan. Arrange boerewors slices on top and allow to set over gentle heat. Place omelette under grill and allow to brown slightly.
SERVES 2

BOEREWORS AND RICE DISH

1 onion, sliced
10 mℓ butter
2 baby marrows, sliced
100 g whole button mushrooms, wiped
2 tomatoes, cubed
5 mℓ salt
1 mℓ sweet basil
freshly ground black pepper to taste
300 g hot, cooked boerewors
250 mℓ hot, cooked rice

Sauté the onion in heated butter. Add baby marrows, mushrooms, tomatoes and seasonings and simmer until just tender. Slice boerewors into 25-mm slices, combine with hot rice, then pour vegetable mixture over. Serve immediately.
SERVES 4

RUSSIAN SAUSAGE AND BANANA KEBABS

2 Russian sausages
1 banana
4 rashers rindless, streaky bacon

BASTING MIXTURE
15 mℓ honey
1 mℓ ground ginger
5 mℓ lemon juice

Slice sausages and banana into 25-mm pieces. Cut bacon into smaller pieces and wrap around each piece of banana. Thread banana and sausages alternately onto skewers. Mix together the ingredients for the basting mixture. Grill the kebabs, basting frequently with the honey mixture, until bacon is crisp and sausages are heated through.
SERVES 2

SAUSAGE STIR-FRY

125 g Vienna sausages, sliced
125 g frankfurters, sliced
150 g Russian sausages, sliced
30 mℓ cooking oil
1 clove garlic, crushed
1 large onion, thinly sliced
2 carrots, cut julienne
1 green pepper, cut into strips
3 baby marrows, sliced
300 g mushrooms, sliced
1 x 410-g can pineapple pieces
5 mℓ salt
freshly ground black pepper to taste
2 mℓ ground ginger
15 mℓ soy sauce
30 mℓ wine vinegar
30 mℓ cornflour

Brown sausages in heated cooking oil in a heavy-based saucepan or wok. Add garlic, onion, carrots and green pepper and stir-fry for 2 minutes. Add baby marrows and mushrooms and stir-fry 2 minutes more. Drain pineapple pieces, reserving the syrup, and add. Season sausages and vegetables with salt, pepper and ginger. Combine reserved pineapple syrup, soy sauce, vinegar and cornflour. Stir into stir-fry and bring to the boil. Simmer until thickened, then serve immediately with rice.
SERVES 4

SALAMI AND NOODLE SALAD

2 tomatoes, quartered
250 mℓ cooked ribbon noodles, cooled
2 small green peppers, thinly sliced
10 thin slices salami
2 mℓ dried oregano
freshly ground black pepper to taste
30 mℓ cooking oil
15 mℓ wine vinegar
1 clove garlic, crushed
8 stuffed olives (optional)

In a salad bowl, arrange tomatoes, noodles, green pepper and salami and season with oregano and pepper. Mix oil, vinegar and garlic together and pour over salad. If using, arrange olives on top of salad and serve.
SERVES 4

SAVOURY SALAMI TARTLETS

1 onion, chopped
10 mℓ butter
1 clove garlic, crushed
200 g cauliflower, divided into florets
250 g salami, cut into strips
200 g ready-made puff pastry

SAUCE
30 mℓ butter
30 mℓ cake flour
250 mℓ warm milk
50 mℓ cream
2 mℓ mustard powder
1 mℓ salt
freshly ground black pepper to taste
100 g Cheddar cheese, grated (250 mℓ)

Sauté onion in heated butter until transparent. Add garlic, cauliflower and salami and stir-fry for 2 minutes. Roll out pastry and line muffin pans. Prick the base of the pastry, then bake blind for 7 minutes at 200 °C.

To make the sauce: Melt butter, remove from heat and stir in flour. Return to heat and cook for 1 minute. Slowly add warm milk, stirring continuously until sauce thickens. Remove from heat and stir in cream, mustard, salt and pepper. Add salami and cauliflower mixture to sauce. Leave to cool, then spoon into pastry shells, sprinkle with cheese and bake for 10-15 minutes at 200 °C. Serve as a starter or light lunch.
MAKES 18 TARTLETS

VARIATION
This salami mixture makes a delicious filling for omelettes or pancakes.

TROPICAL SANDWICHES

250 mℓ chopped salami
75 mℓ chopped almonds
75 mℓ chopped gherkins
125 mℓ mayonnaise
6 slices bread
6 slices pineapple
50 g Cheddar cheese, grated (125 mℓ)
6 rashers bacon, crisply fried

Mix salami, almonds, gherkins and mayonnaise and spread an equal amount on each slice of bread. Top each with a slice of pineapple and a sprinkling of cheese. Grill until the cheese has melted, then garnish with crisply fried bacon.
SERVES 6

SAUSAGE AND APPLE PLAIT

SOUR CREAM PASTRY
240 g cake flour (500 mℓ)
2 mℓ salt
125 g butter
100 mℓ sour cream

FILLING
30 mℓ prepared mustard
250 g cooking apples, peeled and coarsely chopped
1 onion, coarsely chopped
5 mℓ salt
freshly ground black pepper to taste
15 mℓ freshly chopped sage or 5 mℓ dried
8 pork sausages, cooked and sliced
1 egg, beaten

To make the pastry: Sift flour and salt together. Cut butter into cubes and rub into flour until mixture resembles fine bread-crumbs. Add sour cream and mix to a stiff dough. Wrap in grease-proof paper and refrigerate for about 1 hour.

Roll pastry out thinly into a rectangle. Spread mustard over pastry, leaving 25 mm clear round the edges. Arrange apples, onion and seasonings in a narrow strip down length of pastry. Arrange sausages on top and brush edges of pastry with beaten egg. Make diagonal cuts, 80 mm long and 30 mm apart, in the pastry as shown. Fold top part of pastry over filling, then plait the pastry strips as shown. Fold bottom part of pastry over filling, place pastry plait on a greased baking sheet and brush with remaining beaten egg. Bake in a preheated 200 °C oven for 30-35 minutes until golden brown.
SERVES 4

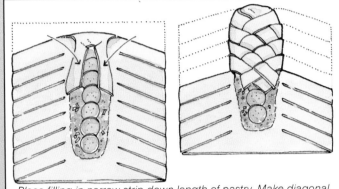

Place filling in narrow strip down length of pastry. Make diagonal cuts, then plait the pastry strips as shown above.

From left to right: Sausage and apple plait, Salami and noodle salad, Sausage stir-fry and (foreground) Savoury salami tartlets

Cured and smoked meats

Until the last century, curing was used for preservation, but is now used primarily for the development of flavour and colour.

There are two basic methods of curing, namely dry curing and wet curing. In dry curing, the cure is rubbed into the meat by hand while in the latter method the meat is soaked in a mixture of water and curing agents. Although dry curing is faster, it results in high mass loss and is now considered old-fashioned. Commercially-prepared curing mixtures are available which reduce the curing period considerably – the meat is ready for cooking or smoking six to seven hours after injecting the curing mixture into the meat by means of a perforated needle, or two to five days after immersion.

Apart from the preserving effect smoking has on meat, it also gives it a unique flavour and a rich brown colour. Whether done on a commercial or a home scale, the technique of smoking involves hanging the meat or placing it on racks in a chamber designed to contain the smoke. Depending on the thickness of the meat and the type of meat being smoked, the smoking period may vary from as short as a few minutes to several hours or even days.

PORK

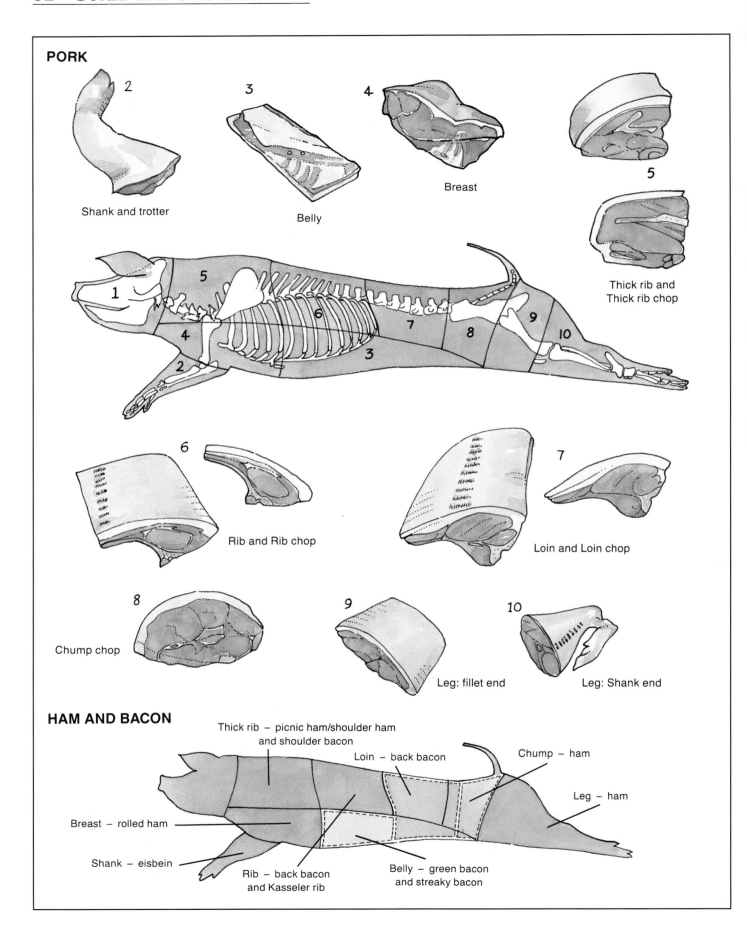

2
Shank and trotter

3
Belly

4
Breast

5
Thick rib and Thick rib chop

6
Rib and Rib chop

7
Loin and Loin chop

8
Chump chop

9
Leg: fillet end

10
Leg: Shank end

HAM AND BACON

Thick rib – picnic ham/shoulder ham and shoulder bacon

Loin – back bacon

Chump – ham

Leg – ham

Breast – rolled ham

Shank – eisbein

Rib – back bacon and Kasseler rib

Belly – green bacon and streaky bacon

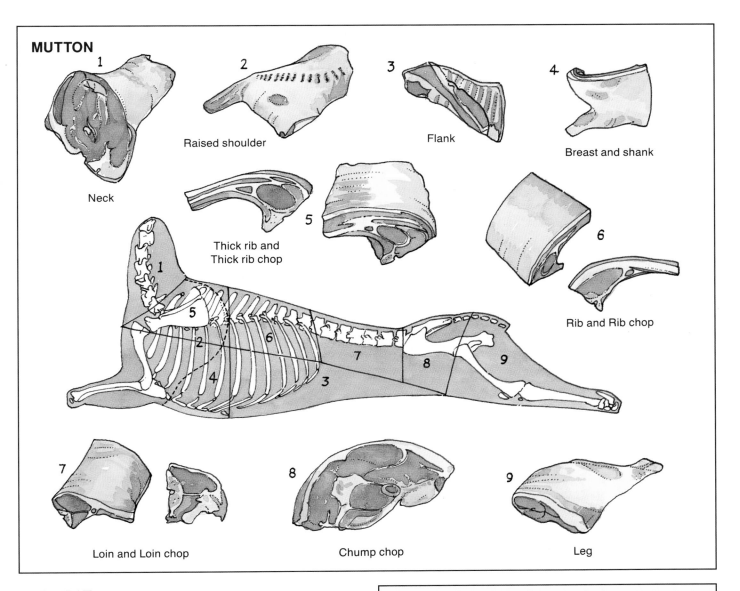

MUTTON

1 Neck

2 Raised shoulder

3 Flank

4 Breast and shank

5 Thick rib and Thick rib chop

6 Rib and Rib chop

7 Loin and Loin chop

8 Chump chop

9 Leg

THE MEAT

Lamb and mutton
Although lamb or mutton is not normally cured and smoked, traditional Soutribbetjie *(see page 40)*, made from the breast section, and Leipoldt ham (mock ham) are made with lamb. For those who don't eat pork, Leipoldt ham is a tasty alternative. Made from leg of mutton or lamb, this 'ham' is cured and smoked according to a special recipe created by the poet Louis Leipoldt *(see page 40)*.

Pork
Theoretically every kind of meat can be cured, but pork has long been the prime candidate because this fine-textured meat responds so positively to curing. Almost the entire pork carcase can be cured or cured and smoked. The leg is normally used for hams, but other cuts such as the shoulder (shoulder ham) and thick rib (picnic ham) are also suitable. The rib, loin and belly may be used for bacon and the rib for Kasseler ribs while cured pork shank and trotters are ideal for soups and stews. Smoked speck is used for larding and the skin can be added to soups and stews for extra flavour.

SPECK AND BACON
It is necessary to distinguish between speck and bacon. Bacon refers to cured and smoked pork, with the exception of green bacon (which is unsmoked), while speck refers to pork or mutton fat. Green bacon can be identified by its pale pink flesh and off-white to dark cream rind. Smoked bacon, on the other hand, has a golden rind and deep pink flesh.

Beef
Cured brisket and silverside are more commonly known as corned beef, while cured beef covered with a highly spiced mixture available from spice merchants, is known as pastrami. Cured and smoked silverside is known as smoked beef and, unlike corned beef and pastrami which require further cooking after curing, is eaten raw, cut into paper-thin slices.

NOTE
☐ It is important to bear in mind that the better the quality of the meat, the better the end product.

Plastic, wooden, enamel, stainless steel or earthenware containers are ideal for wet curing.

CURING CONTAINERS

Containers should be made of plastic, wood, enamel or earthenware. Avoid metal and cracked enamel containers as the curing mixture reacts with the metal causing discoloration and a strange taste. A small wooden barrel is ideal for wet curing, but if it has been used previously for something else, it should be cleaned thoroughly to remove any lingering taste.

The container best suited to wet curing is one that is tall and upright as this shape can hold the maximum amount of meat with the minimum quantity of brine. For dry curing, a shallow, flat container will suffice.

Curing barrels of asbestos or cement are available commercially. These are particularly suitable for use during winter months in a cool climate as they keep the curing mixture cold without refrigeration.

CURING INGREDIENTS

The basic ingredients of a home cure are salt, saltpetre, sugar, bicarbonate of soda, spices and, for wet curing, water.

Salt is the active preservation agent and gives cured meat its specific taste. Clean, coarse salt (dairy salt) is best for home curing although fine salt is generally used in commercial mixtures. If using fine salt, reduce the amount given in the tables by half to prevent the meat being too salty. The quantity of salt added to the curing mixture of hams will determine whether they should be termed 'sweet', 'medium' or 'strong'. Sweet hams tend to be the most popular for cooking purposes, while strong hams, being very salty, are ideal for long storage.

Saltpetre imparts an attractive pink colour to the meat and helps to inhibit bacterial growth. Use it sparingly as too much saltpetre will toughen the meat and harden the fibres. It can be omitted if a less pronounced colour effect is desired.

CURING MIXTURES FOR BEEF			
MEAT	50 kg	25 kg	2,5-12 kg
WATER	20 ℓ	10 ℓ	5 ℓ
DAIRY SALT	3 kg	1,5 kg	750 g
SALTPETRE	90 kg	45 g	25 g
SUGAR	360 g	180 g	90 g
BICARBONATE OF SODA	120 g	60 g	30 g

SPICES	
Mixture A	Mixture B
For every 25 kg meat	For every 25 kg meat
16 bay leaves 24 whole allspice 12 white peppercorns 2 cinnamon sticks 20 mℓ mustard powder 3-6 cloves garlic, crushed (optional)	5 mℓ black peppercorns 24 bay leaves 24 whole allspice 30 mℓ ground ginger 3-6 cloves garlic, crushed (optional)

CURING MIXTURES FOR PORK				
MEAT	up to 5 kg	5-15 kg	15-25 kg	25-50 kg
WATER	5 ℓ	10 ℓ	15 ℓ	20 ℓ
SALTPETRE	45-60 g	90-120 g	140-180 g	180-240 g
SUGAR	60 g	120 g	180 g	240 g
Salt for: SWEET HAMS, BACON AND KASSELER RIB	950 g	1,9 kg	2,85 kg	3,2 kg
MEDIUM HAMS	1,1 kg	2,2 kg	3,3 kg	4,3 kg
STRONG HAMS	1,3 kg	2,3 kg	3,6 kg	4,75 kg
Spices: BLACK PEPPER	30 g	60 g	90 g	120 g
WHOLE ALLSPICE	30 g	60 g	90 g	120 g
WHOLE CORIANDER	45 g	90 g	135 g	180 g

CURING MIXTURES FOR MUTTON	
LEIPOLDT HAM	SOUTRIBBETJIE
Large leg of mutton	1-1,5 kg breast of lamb
500 g coarse salt 30 g saltpetre 120 g brown sugar 60 g pepper 30 g coriander	1 ℓ water 225 g coarse salt 10 mℓ saltpetre 30 g sugar 10 mℓ bicarbonate of soda

Stretch meat netting is obtainable from your butcher and is ideal for keeping boned meat in shape during curing, smoking or cooking.

Sugar counteracts the toughening effect of salt and adds to the flavour. Although yellow or brown sugar is tastier than white, it should never be moist as this causes the curing mixture to foam and the meat to spoil. If you do not have any dry brown sugar available, mix it with a little white sugar until the texture becomes loose and does not compress under hand pressure. In very hot climates, especially where humidity is high, it is advisable to use only white sugar.

Bicarbonate of soda is often added to the curing mixture to inhibit spoilage, especially in hot areas.

Spices help to improve the flavour of the meat and are usually added according to personal taste. Combinations of some or all of the following seasonings are most commonly used: pepper, bay leaves, whole cloves, whole allspice, cinnamon sticks, whole coriander, garlic, ground ginger and mustard powder. Premixed curing spices are also available from spice dealers.

Water should always be pre-boiled. This helps to dissolve the curing ingredients more easily and also serves to sterilize the cure to prevent spoilage.

WET CURING

Conventional method

Pre-boil the water, add the salt, sugar and saltpetre and/or bicarbonate of soda, stir well to dissolve, then pour through a muslin cloth into the curing barrel. Wrap the whole spices in a piece of muslin and add. When the mixture is cool, add the meat. Make sure that there is enough brine to cover all the meat and remember to turn it every day during the curing period.

NOTE

☐ If the meat floats in the curing mixture, weigh it down with a heavy non-metallic weight.

Curing times

Pork: The curing period for pork is calculated on the penetration rate of the brine into the meat, that is, 25 mm in two days. Remember that boned meat (and especially the leg and thick rib) requires about half the curing time needed for meat with the bone intact. For example, the curing time for a 7 kg leg of pork on the bone is four to six days; when boned, this time is reduced to three to five days. The curing time for shoulder hams (if boned) and for bacon is about three to four days.

Beef and Lamb: Meat less than 75 mm thick should be cured for two to three days. Thicker cuts should be left in the curing mixture for longer.

QUICK CURING

To reduce the curing time, the mixture can be injected into the meat with a curing syringe. The quantity of curing mixture required is about a quarter of the meat's own mass. Insert the needle into the meat in the same direction as the grain of the meat. Leave the meat in the remaining mixture for one day per 2 kg of meat until ready for cooking or smoking. Clean the syringe thoroughly after use and store the parts separately.

Commercial mixtures

Commercially prepared curing mixtures reduce the curing period to such a degree that the meat is ready for cooking six to seven hours after injection or two to five days after immersion. These mixtures can be ordered by brand name from merchants supplying butchers' requirements and have their own directions for use. In some instances, the same mixture can be used for both beef and pork.

TO RE-USE WET CURING MIXTURE

The wet curing mixture can be re-used if it is boiled and the salt replenished. Bring the mixture to the boil, remove from the stove and, using a salinometer to calculate the salt concentration, add more salt until the salinometer registers between 15-17 degrees or parts per thousand (depending on the type of salinometer being used). If a salinometer is not available, drop a potato or fresh egg (in the shell) into the curing solution, and gradually add salt until the potato or egg rises to the surface. This simple method works well and is ideal for preparing curing mixtures at home.

To shorten the curing time, inject the curing mixture into the meat with a curing syringe.

DRY CURING

Using the same ingredients as for wet curing but omitting the water, calculate the quantity required at about 30-45 g per 500 g of meat. Combine the salt, saltpetre, sugar, and bicarbonate of soda and spices and mix well. Rub the mixture into the meat, transfer it to a suitable container, placing the thicker pieces at the bottom (if more than one is being cured), and sprinkle the remaining curing mixture over. Keep the meat refrigerated and rub the mixture into the meat every day. For meat cuts less than 75 mm thick, allow two days per 500 g and for thicker cuts, allow two to three days per 500 g.

STORAGE DURING THE CURING PROCESS

Except in very cold climates, it is best to store the curing meat in a refrigerator or cold room at temperatures ranging from 2 °C to 4 °C. Although meat can be cured successfully in cold rooms between 4 °C and 10 °C, temperatures outside this range will have an adverse effect on the curing. If there are any signs of mould or putrefaction, immediately remove the meat from the curing mixture and wipe the meat all over with a cloth wrung out in vinegar. Bring the curing mixture to the boil, then allow to cool before replacing the meat. If necessary, prepare a new curing mixture.

SMOKING MEAT AND SAUSAGES

Before smoking, place the meat in fresh water for 30 minutes to flush out the extra salt, then hang the meat or place it on a wire rack for at least 24 hours to allow the outer surface to dry. Sausages need only be hung up to dry before being smoked. Meat that has not dried off sufficiently seldom gets that characteristic golden colour that smoking imparts.

THE SMOKER

Several types of smoker can be built by the do-it-yourselfer – from the most simple, an empty drum, to a proper smoking oven usually forming part of an outside braai area. Instructions for the construction of a drum smoker and a smoking chamber are given below.

Position the smoker in a sheltered, shady spot. Too strong a draught may affect the smoke while sun baking down on the smoker may increase the temperature inside and spoil the meat.

Drum smokers

Remove the base and lid of a 100-ℓ drum and clean it thoroughly, using detergent and disinfectant. Fix one or more horizontal bars to the inside of the drum (about 75 mm from the top) on which to hang the meat. These bars can be welded to the drum or inserted into slots cut into the sides of the drum.

Build a foundation by stacking a double layer of bricks (about 16) for the drum to stand on. Leave an opening in the top layer of bricks for lighting the sawdust. The air draught can be controlled by placing a plank over the opening. Pack damp earth around the outer edge of the bricks and drum to make the whole assembly airtight. Cover the top of the drum with a wet sack or a flat sheet, raising it slightly to allow the smoke to escape by

inserting two pieces of wood (about 5 mm thick) between the drum and the sheet. If slots have been made to accommodate the bars, these will be sufficient to let out the smoke and it will not be necessary to raise the cover.

Instead of the brick foundation, the drum can be extended by welding a half drum, also open at both ends, to the bottom of the main drum. Saw an opening, measuring 100-125 mm, into the base of the drum as shown. Air draughts can again be controlled by means of a door or plank placed over the opening.

The smoking chamber

A smoking chamber can be built of brick with a concrete floor and tight-fitting door. The size of the chamber may vary, but a convenient guide is 1,5 x 1,5 x 2 metres. For ventilation the roof should have a chimney and at the base of the chamber there should be an opening of about 25 mm x 600 mm. Make provision for hanging the meat by building steel bars into the walls. These can be placed at two different heights, about 500 mm apart.

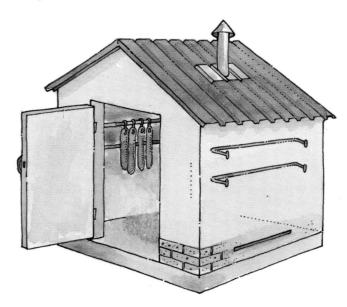

THE SAWDUST

Sawdust from hard, non-resinous types of wood, such as black wattle and walnut, is usually used for smoking purposes. Mealie stalks, vine stalks and sunflower hay make adequate substitutes but smoking with wood requires the least attention and gives the best results. Sprigs of herbs, soaked in water for 10 minutes, then drained and placed on top of the sawdust will add interest to both the aroma and the flavour of the meat.

SMOKING THE MEAT

In the centre of the smoking chamber or drum floor, place about 2 kg of sawdust in a heap measuring about 600 mm in diameter by 120 mm high. Make a hollow in the middle of the pile of sawdust and set it alight with kindling or crumpled newspaper. Leave the door ajar until the sawdust starts to smoulder well, then hang up the meat and shut the door tightly so that the smoking process can begin. Make sure that the meat is not too near the heat source and that the cuts are not touching. Use strong biltong hooks if there aren't any loops to hang it by.

NOTE
☐ The sawdust should smoulder, never flame.

Smoking times

Smoking times are difficult to predict since other factors such as the outside temperature, wind, the type of smoking apparatus used and so on influence these times. As you gain more experience in smoking meat, you will be able to judge more accurately when the meat is ready, but a good guideline is to use the recommended quantity of sawdust (2 kg) and to allow it to burn out completely; this should create enough smoke for even the larger cuts. If the meat has not gone a rich golden brown after the first smoking – as sometimes happens with ham and bacon – it can be cooled down completely and then smoked a second time. Sausages and biltong on the other hand often have to be removed before the sawdust burns out as they are ready sooner than large cuts of meat.

STORAGE

Before refrigerating any smoked meat, leave it to cool down to room temperature. A 5 kg ham, for instance, will take at least 24 hours to reach room temperature, so calculate the cooling times for other cuts accordingly.

Once a whole ham has cooled to room temperature, it can be wrapped in mutton cloth or a sheet of transparent aluminium foil (not the usual 'tin foil' since this will react chemically with the curing mixture causing holes in the aluminium), and refrigerated. Stored this way it will keep for about three weeks.

Sliced ham or corned meat can be wrapped in transparent aluminium foil or stored in airtight containers and refrigerated for about five days.

Freezing for periods longer than a month will cause changes in both the taste and the texture of the meat.

Parma-style hams go through a seven month drying period during which time they are alternately pressed and hung up to dry.

HOW TO TIE A BONED LEG OR SHOULDER
Before boned meat can be smoked or cooked, it should first be tied.

1. Sprinkle about 30 g of dry gelatine over the inside of the meat. This prevents the meat falling apart during cooking and carving.

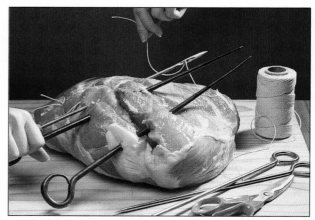

2. Fold the rump section over to cover the opening furthest from the shank and secure with string.

3. Sew up the shank end and tie the string criss-cross fashion as shown, making a loop for hanging the meat during the smoking process. Alternatively, the meat may be placed in a special bag obtainable from spice dealers.

After a four-week curing period, these Westphalian hams are smoked for four days in a commercial smoker (top), then air-dried in the curing room for a further three weeks (bottom).

Unlike smoked beef, some meats, such as ham, corned beef and pastrami, still require further cooking once they have been cured or cured and smoked.

HAM

There are various methods of cooking large hams, but boiling is by far the most common. If you don't have a large enough sauce-pan in which to boil the ham, it can be baked in foil.

Boiling a ham

Place the cured and smoked ham in a saucepan, cover with cold water and add 1-2 carrots, 1 large onion stuck with 4 whole cloves, 1 sprig parsley, 1 bay leaf, 5 black peppercorns, 5 mℓ mustard powder and 15 mℓ brown sugar. Bring the liquid to the boil, then lower the temperature, cover the pan with its lid and simmer until the meat is tender, allowing about 30 minutes per 500 g or until a piece of meat can be pulled away easily. To ensure a more succulent ham, leave it to cool in the cooking liquid before removing the outer skin. Score the outer fat layer in a diamond pattern and spoon over the glaze *(see pages 42 & 43)* of your choice. Bake at 160 °C for 30 minutes, spooning over the remaining glaze at regular intervals.

VARIATIONS

For extra flavour, add the skin of a pineapple or 350 mℓ pineapple juice, apple juice or apple cider to the pan while the meat is simmering.

Baking a ham in foil

Wrap the meat in a large sheet of aluminium foil, shiny side in, and roast at 160 °C for 15-20 minutes per 500 g meat. Remove meat from foil and pull off the outer skin, leaving the outer layer of fat intact. Score the outer fat layer in a diamond pattern, place the meat on the rack of a roasting pan and spoon over half the glaze. Bake at 160 °C for a further 30 minutes, spooning over the remaining glaze at regular intervals.

Microwaving a ham

In a suitable container, bring to the boil enough water and fruit juice to cover the ham. Add the meat together with 4 whole cloves, 1 sprig parsley, 1 bay leaf, 5 black peppercorns and 5 mℓ mustard powder and cover with a lid or cling wrap. Microwave on 70% for 10-12 minutes per 500 g, then remove the meat from the liquid, pull off the outer skin and score the outer fat layer in a diamond pattern. Arrange whole cloves, glacé cherries or pineapple rings on top and prepare the glaze of your choice. Microwave the ham, uncovered, on 70% for a further 5-6 minutes per 500 g, basting with glaze every 5 minutes. Leave to stand for 20 minutes before serving.

HINTS
- If you are unsure of quantities, allow 110-160 g boneless raw meat or 160-225 g meat on the bone per person.
- When cooking a large piece of meat you may find yourself with lots of leftover meat. Freezing will spoil the flavour so use leftovers as suggested in the recipes given below.
- When carving cold ham or corned beef, keep the slices as thin as possible: two or three thin slices are more appetizing than one thick slice, especially in sandwiches.
- If you suspect that the uncooked ham or corned beef is too salty, soak it overnight in cold water, pour off the water and use fresh water for boiling. If the meat still tastes too salty, again pour off the water, cover with fresh cold water and boil a second time.

Score the outer fat layer in a diamond pattern before garnishing and glazing the ham.

From left to right: A selection of cured meats – corned beef, bacon, Leipoldt ham, soutribbetjie and pastrami.

BACON

Although bacon is an inseparable part of the traditional English breakfast and makes a delicious addition to many dishes, few people know how to cook it correctly.

Pan-grilling

Place the bacon in a cold riffle pan and heat gradually. Turn the bacon frequently until grilled to your liking.

Oven-grilling

Place the bacon on the rack of an oven-roasting pan and grill 75 mm below the pre-heated element. Keep the oven door open and grill both sides of the bacon until it is crispy. This method is more practical for large quantities of bacon and for those who are diet conscious.

LEIPOLDT HAM

Select a large leg of mutton and trim it to the shape of a conventional ham. Mix 30 g saltpetre, 120 g brown sugar, 500 g coarse salt, 60 g pepper and 30 g crushed coriander. Rub this mixture over and into the meat, filling the little hollows and cavities, then place it in a wooden trough. Sprinkle with the remaining mixture and leave it to cure for 10 days, rubbing the mixture into the meat and turning it every day. Remove from trough, place a weight on top to expel the curing liquid, and leave for a further 2 days.

The meat is now ready for smoking *(see page 37)*, preferably in smoke from a wood fire (traditionally the leg was hung in a chimney for this purpose) or in a smoker. The smoked mutton 'ham' can be stored in a cool place for 4-5 days before boiling and baking as described.

Cover the cured and smoked leg of mutton with cold water. Add bay leaf, sprig of parsley, peppercorns, 1 onion stuck with 2 cloves and 1 carrot and bring to the boil. Simmer until tender, remove meat from cooking liquid and place on a rack to dry.

For the glaze, mix 10 mℓ mustard powder with 25 mℓ brown sugar and 50 mℓ wine vinegar.

Place the meat on the rack of an oven-roasting pan, brush with half the glazing mixture and oven roast for 30 minutes at 160 °C, brushing the remaining glaze over at regular intervals until a good glaze is obtained.

CORNED BEEF

Follow the directions for boiling ham and cook the beef in the same manner. Serve it cold in sandwiches or hot with carrots and cabbage, and mustard.

PASTRAMI

Place the prepared pastrami in a cooking bag and cook at 160 °C for 25-30 minutes per 500 g, plus an extra 25-30 minutes. Serve hot or cold with a mustard sauce and vegetables or salads or, thinly sliced, in sandwiches.

SOUTRIBBETJIE

Ask your butcher to saw through the breast bone of a 1-1,5 kg breast of lamb so that the meat can more easily be cut into serving portions. Bring 1 ℓ water to the boil and add 225 g coarse salt, 10 mℓ saltpetre, 30 g sugar and 10 mℓ bicarbonate of soda, stirring well until dissolved. Allow the liquid to cool, then strain it through a muslin cloth into a glass, earthenware or plastic container. Add the meat and leave for 2 days in a cool spot or in the refrigerator. Remove the meat from the liquid and hang it in a well-ventilated spot until dried.

Place the ribbetjie in a saucepan, cover with cold water and bring to the boil. Reduce the heat and simmer for 1½ hours or until the meat is almost tender. Let it cool in the cooking liquid, then hang it in a cool place to dry. Grill the ribbetjie over moderate coals for about 10 minutes, until brown and crisp. Cut into serving portions and serve with lemon wedges.
SERVES 6

VARIATION
Dry curing is the more traditional method of salting ribbetjies. Mix together the salt, saltpetre, sugar and bicarbonate of soda and, using 30-45 g per 500 g meat, rub the dry mixture into the meat. Place the ribbetjies in a glass, earthenware or plastic container, laying the thicker pieces at the bottom of the dish, and refrigerate for 2-3 days. Hang the meat in a cool, well-ventilated place to dry, then boil and grill as described above. Once boiled, the rib will keep for up to a week if covered in a muslin cloth and left to hang in a well-ventilated spot.

STEP-BY-STEP

1. Prepare the curing mixture by boiling the water and adding the curing ingredients. Allow to cool.

2. If the meat has been boned, sprinkle it with dry gelatine and tie it with string to hold its shape.

3. Add the meat, making sure there is enough brine to cover the meat completely, then place the curing barrel in a cool place.

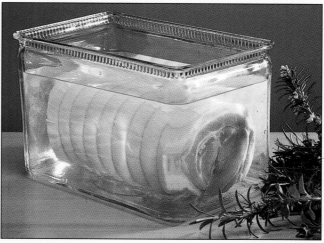

4. When the curing period is over, place the meat in fresh water for 30 minutes, then hang it up for at least 24 hours to dry.

5. Ignite the sawdust in the smoking drum or chamber and when it is smouldering, hang up the meat.

6. When the smoking is complete, allow the meat to return to room temperature before refrigerating.

APPLE AND ORANGE GLAZE

1 x 410 g can apples, mashed
30 mℓ brandy
juice of 1 orange
50 mℓ breadcrumbs
5 mℓ grated orange rind

Combine all the ingredients and mix well. Spoon half the mixture over the ham and bake at 160 °C for 30 minutes. Spoon remaining glaze over at regular intervals while baking the ham.

APRICOT GLAZE

250 mℓ chopped canned apricots
50 mℓ brown sugar
5 mℓ ground ginger

Combine all the ingredients and mix well. Spoon half the mixture over the ham and bake at 160 °C for 30 minutes. Spoon remaining glaze over at regular intervals while baking the ham.

APRICOT JAM GLAZE

100 mℓ smooth apricot jam
2 mℓ dry mustard
15 mℓ vinegar
15 mℓ cooking oil

Combine all the ingredients, mixing well. Spoon half the mixture over the ham and bake at 160 °C for 30 minutes. Spoon remaining glaze over at regular intervals while baking the ham.

PRUNE AND APRICOT GLAZE

250 g prunes, stoned
100 mℓ black tea
50 mℓ brandy
1 stick cinnamon
1 x 439 g can apricots, drained and crushed
5 mℓ ground ginger
2 mℓ ground cloves

Soak prunes in black tea for two hours, then drain, reserving the liquid. Make deep incisions in the fat of the ham and press the prunes into the cuts. Mix prune liquid with the remaining ingredients and spoon half over the ham during the last 30 minutes of cooking time. Spoon remaining glaze over at regular intervals.

PINEAPPLE GLAZE

1 x 439-g can pineapple rings
15 mℓ melted butter
15-30 mℓ cake flour
50 mℓ sherry
7 mℓ prepared mustard

Drain the pineapple rings, reserving the juice, and arrange on the cooked meat. Mix the butter and flour to a paste and gradually stir in 125 mℓ of the reserved pineapple juice. Add the sherry and mustard and stir over low heat until thickened.

MUSTARD GLAZE

50 mℓ prepared mustard
50 mℓ brown sugar
50 mℓ vinegar
30 mℓ honey

Combine all the ingredients, mixing well. Spoon half the mixture over the ham and bake at 160 °C for 30 minutes. Spoon remaining glaze over at regular intervals while baking the ham.

APPLE JELLY GLAZE

250 mℓ apple jelly
1 mℓ ground cloves
1 mℓ ground cinnamon
1 mℓ grated nutmeg

Combine all the ingredients, mixing well. Spoon half the mixture over the ham and bake at 160 °C for 30 minutes. Spoon remaining glaze over at regular intervals while baking the ham.

VARIATION
Substitute redcurrant or quince jelly for the apple jelly.
Spoon half the mixture over the ham and bake at 160 °C for 30 minutes. Spoon remaining glaze over at regular intervals while baking the ham.

BEER GLAZE

1 onion, chopped
60 g brown sugar
5 mℓ French mustard
2 mℓ dried mixed herbs
125 mℓ beer

Combine all the ingredients and simmer for 10 minutes. Spoon half the mixture over the ham and bake at 160 °C for 30 minutes. Spoon remaining glaze over at regular intervals while baking the ham.

HAM AND CHEESE QUICHE
(Microwave)

PASTRY BASE
75 g butter, melted
150 g cake flour (300 mℓ)
pinch of salt
1 egg, beaten
30 mℓ cold water

FILLING
2 eggs, beaten
150 mℓ milk
100 mℓ cream
5 mℓ prepared mustard
150 g cooked ham, chopped
100 g Gruyère or Cheddar cheese, grated (250 mℓ)

To make the pastry: Rub the butter into the flour until the mixture is crumbly. Add salt, egg and water and mix to a soft dough. Roll out into a circle. Place dough in a greased quiche dish and prick well with a fork. Place paper towel on top, followed by dried beans or raw rice and microwave on 100% for 3 minutes. Remove paper and beans or rice and microwave for a further 1-2 minutes.

To make the filling: Mix the eggs, milk, cream and mustard in a separate container and microwave on 100% for 3-5 minutes, stirring frequently to prevent it from boiling over. Add ham and half the cheese and mix. Pour mixture into pastry case and microwave on 50% for about 6 minutes. Sprinkle remaining cheese over and microwave for 1 minute more.
SERVES 8

VARIATION
Substitute chopped salami, frankfurters or any other processed meats for the ham.

HAM AND CHEDDAR BAVAROISE

1,5 ℓ milk
6 egg yolks, beaten
20 mℓ gelatine
120 mℓ milk
300 mℓ Cheddar cheese, grated
15 slices cooked ham, chopped
50 mℓ chopped chives
400 mℓ thickened cream, whipped

GARNISH
green and black peppercorns, crushed
6 chives

Heat 1,5 ℓ milk almost to boiling point, add egg yolks and stir over low heat until mixture thickens. Do not boil. Cool covered. Soften gelatine in 120 mℓ milk and heat over boiling water until dissolved. Add to cooled custard mixture and mix thoroughly. Add cheese, ham and chives. When mixture is completely cold, fold in the whipped cream. Pour into greased dariole moulds and chill several hours or overnight. Unmould carefully (mixture will be soft), sprinkle with crushed peppercorns and garnish with whole chives. Serve as an hors d'oeuvre with crudités or sliced apple and crusty bread.
SERVES 6

Clockwise from right: Corned hump with fruit and mustard sauce, Ham salad, Ham and cheese quiche and Ham and Cheddar bavaroise

HAM AND POTATO PANCAKES

4 large potatoes (about 1 kg)
250 g cooked ham, finely chopped
25 mℓ cooking oil
25 mℓ butter

Peel potatoes and grate coarsely into cold, salted water. Drain, and squeeze moisture out of grated potato, blot dry on paper towel and mix with ham. In a non-stick frying pan, heat half the oil and butter and dot small amounts of mixture into hot fat. Fry over medium heat for about 3 minutes, pushing down firmly with an egglifter. Turn pancakes over and fry for a further 3-5 minutes or until cooked through. Drain and serve hot.
SERVES 6-8

HAM SALAD

450 g cooked ham, cubed
1 large tomato, quartered
3 gherkins, sliced
½ onion, sliced
½ head red cos lettuce

SALAD DRESSING
50 mℓ mayonnaise
30 mℓ milk
2 mℓ salt
freshly ground black pepper to taste

First make the salad dressing by combining all the ingredients thoroughly, and refrigerate. Arrange salad ingredients in salad bowl. Just before serving, pour salad dressing over salad or serve separately.
SERVES 4

CORNED HUMP WITH FRUIT AND MUSTARD SAUCE

1 corned hump
4 whole cloves
1 onion
1 carrot
2 bay leaves

FRUIT AND MUSTARD SAUCE
1 onion, sliced
10 mℓ cooking oil
50 mℓ smooth apricot jam
500 mℓ water
125 g dried apricots
125 g dried apple rings
20 mℓ prepared English mustard
30 mℓ French mustard
5 mℓ chopped fresh root ginger

Place meat in a saucepan and cover with cold water. Insert cloves in onion and add to meat together with carrot and bay leaves. Bring to the boil, reduce heat and simmer for 2-2½ hours or until meat is tender.

If meat is to be served hot, remove meat from liquid, slice thinly and serve with fruit and mustard sauce. If serving cold, allow meat to cool in the cooking liquid.

To make the sauce: Sauté the onion in heated cooking oil. Remove from heat, add apricot jam and stir. Add water and stir to dissolve the jam. Add remaining ingredients and simmer approximately 10 minutes until fruit is tender but still firm.
SERVES 6

HAM AND CHEDDAR ROLLS

12 thin slices white bread, crusts removed
25 mℓ prepared mild mustard
200 g cooked ham, finely chopped
200 g mature Cheddar cheese, finely grated (500 mℓ)
freshly ground black pepper to taste
100 g butter

Spread a little mustard onto each slice of bread. Mix the ham and cheese, season with pepper, then spread the mixture on the bread. With the help of a clean, damp dish towel, roll up each slice Swiss roll fashion, and secure with toothpicks. Heat butter in a large frying pan and fry rolls gently until brown. Drain on paper towel, remove toothpicks and serve hot.
SERVES 6

VARIATION
Mozzarella cheese may be substituted for the Cheddar.

SPAGHETTI AND HAM CASSEROLE

500 g cooked ham, cubed
240 g spaghetti, cooked and drained
20 g butter (25 mℓ)
2 cloves garlic, chopped
12 g cake flour (25 mℓ)
500 mℓ milk
25 mℓ chopped parsley
5 mℓ salt
freshly ground black pepper to taste

Combine the ham and spaghetti in a greased casserole. Melt butter in a saucepan, add garlic and sauté. Blend in flour, gradually stir in heated milk and cook until thick and smooth, stirring constantly. Stir in the parsley, salt and pepper and pour over spaghetti mixture. Bake in a pre-heated 160 °C oven for about 35 minutes or until bubbly.
SERVES 6

KASSELER RIB WITH MUSTARD

1,5 kg Kasseler rib chops, 20-mm thick
15 m*ℓ* cooking oil

BASTING SAUCE
10 m*ℓ* brown sugar
50 m*ℓ* wine vinegar
60 m*ℓ* prepared mustard
30 m*ℓ* chopped fresh mixed herbs or 10 m*ℓ* dried

First make the basting sauce by mixing all the ingredients together. Brush meat lightly with cooking oil. Grill over low coals for 7-10 minutes, basting meat regularly with basting sauce.
SERVES 6

Clockwise from right: Kasseler rib with mustard, Ham and Cheddar rolls, Quick bacon and egg pie and Spaghetti and ham casserole

QUICK BACON AND EGG PIE

250 g bacon, rinds removed and quartered
6 leeks, sliced into rings
3 tomatoes, skinned and sliced
6 eggs
125 m*ℓ* milk
500 m*ℓ* fresh breadcrumbs
freshly ground black pepper to taste
2 m*ℓ* salt
5 m*ℓ* mustard powder
100 g Cheddar cheese, grated (250 m*ℓ*)

Place bacon in a cold frying pan. Heat slowly and fry until crisp. Add leeks and fry until transparent. Place bacon and leeks in a greased 270 mm-diameter pie dish. Arrange tomato slices on top. Beat eggs well. Add remaining ingredients, except cheese, and pour over bacon mixture. Sprinkle grated cheese over and bake at 180 °C for about 30 minutes or until the top is golden brown and the mixture set. Serve with a mixed green salad.
SERVES 6

Index

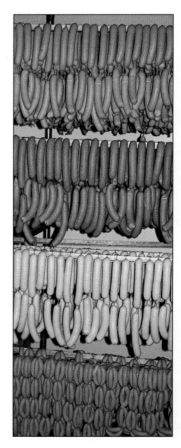

Commercially-made Jumbo frankfurters, Polish sausages, Bratwurst grillers and cocktail franks ready for distribution.